Cool cars

Written by John Lockyer

Lots of us have a car. Some cars are little and some cars are fun. But **cool cars** are the best cars!

Let's have a look at some cool cars. You can see what you think of them.

An American Stock Car

Stock cars run on a track. They might do up to 500 laps if it is a short track.

Stock cars do pit stops, as well. In a pit stop, the car is checked and filled up with gas.

A pit stop

The flag is flapped when the best stock car wins.

High-speed road cars

Cars like this have a **lot** of power. They are some of the quickest cars ever driven on the roads. Speed records for road cars seem to get higher and higher from one year to the next.

The cars are sleek and sit near to the road. Some have an airfoil on the back. An airfoil keeps the tail end of the car down at high speeds.

A big truck

This truck is as big as a tank. It's a big step up to get into the cab.
A truck this big is hard to park. It is not a good car to go to the shops in.

This truck is good on mud roads.
It is good in the sand, too. It can
cross streams with no problems.
But it needs a lot of gas to go.
A gas-guzzler like this costs a lot
to run.

Look up!

Do you think a car has to stick to the road? Not if the car is like this one. It has propellers that can get it into the air. But this car is not allowed to lift off from a road. It has to check in at an airport.

On the airstrip's tarmac, the propellers will pop out and start to spin. When the car is good to go, it lifts off. You can look down at the traffic on the road from the cockpit, as you sail along up high.

Skidding and drifting

This car is seen on mud roads. It kicks up lots of dust. It drifts in soft soil. It skids into corners. It jumps down hills.

The car might crash on a bend. But it has thick bars so it will not be crushed. If it spins off the road, a truck will pull it out. The car might have lots of dents and dings, but that will not stop it.

Jets on a car

This car was a test car. In 1997, it tested out the top speed a car can travel at. The car was not tested on a road. It was tested on a long, flat strip of land in America.

The car had twin jets. The car got 'thrust' from the jets. Thrust is speed and power. The car had wings and a sharp, pointed tip.

In the test, the car zoomed like a rocket. It set the land speed record for a car.

Running on sunlight

Sunlight powers this sort of car. The car has panels on it that collect power from the sun. No gas needs to be put in and no din or smell comes out. It's a 'green' car! 'Green' cars are good for the planet.

Panel to soak up the sun's power

The car can keep the power from the sun, so it can run at night when the sun is not out. Not a lot of sunlight-powered cars have been invented yet.

Electric cars

Electric cars do not get power from the sun, but they are 'green' cars, too. They get power from being plugged into a socket. They help stop smog. That's a good thing.

You can go for a long trip on a short power-up. Just plug in the car for the night in your car port and off you go in the morning.

There are lots of electric cars on the roads today. But they can be hard to hear. To stop them bumping into us, they beep and bleep to tell us that they are near. That's clever.

Classic cars

Classic cars are cars that are 20 to 40 years old. You will see a lot of classic cars at car fairs. They are old, but they are well loved. They will still glimmer and glint in the sun.

Soft tops

A 'soft top' is a sports car with a roof that can be pushed back to let the air in. What a thrill it is to have a trip in a soft top. It's fun to feel the wind in your hair. But you will need to stop and put the top back up if it starts to rain!

Not just a road car

This car can go on the road. And it can go in a river, too. When the car gets to the river bank, you push a button. That starts a propeller. The propeller churns in the river and the car will dip down.

Do not panic – the car has an air tank for you. And the car has no roof, so you can get out in a rush if you need to. The car will sink a little, but not right down to the river bed. Then it will swim along in the river.

You might frighten the fish in this car!

Hot rods

Hot rods are old cars that have been fixed up so that they have extra power and speed. Look at the hot rods at this club. They look good. They have been polished with wax. The rims glitter in the bright sunlight.

Drag cars

Drag cars run on a short track with no bends. A pair of drag cars rev up. They pop, boom and bang. What a racket! When the light turns green, they screech off. They might flip back and stand up. At the end, the quickest drag car wins. Then, the next pair revs up.

23

Now it's your turn. What do you think? Cool or not cool?